Science Sight Word Readers ™

Earth

by Justin McCory Martin

ISBN: 978-0-545-13727-0

Photo Credits: cover: © Bryan Allen/Corbis; title page: © Peter Turner/Getty Images; page 2: © Kevin Horgan/Getty Images; page 3: © Roger Harris/Science Photo Library; page 4: © Roger Harris/Photo Researchers, Inc.; page 4, inset: © Dorling Kindersley RF/Getty Images; page 5: © Stock Connection Distribution/Alamy; page 6: © NASA/Photo Researchers, Inc.; page 7: © Stocktrek RF/Getty Images; page 7, inset: © Richard Newstead/Getty Images; page 8: © Stocktrek RF/Getty Images; page 8, inset: © Frank Krahmer/Photographer's Choice RF/Getty Images; page 9: © Stockbyte RF/Getty Images; page 9, inset: © Andreas Strauss/Getty Images; page 10, from top: © Mark Moffett/Minden Images, © Colin Monteath/Minden Images; page 11, from top: © Konrad Wothe/Minden Images, © Fred Bavendam/Minden Images; page 12: © Tay Rees/Getty Images; page 13: © Peter Turner/Getty Images, page 13, insets from left: © Doug Menuez RF/Getty Images, © George Doyle RF/Getty Images; page 14: © Pete Turner/Getty Images; page 15: © Stocktrek/Getty Images; page 16, from top: © Antonio M. Rosario/Getty Images, © Tom Merton/Getty Images; back cover, from top: © David Jeffery/Getty Images, © Murray Cooper/NPL/Minden Pictures.

Photo research by Dwayne Howard; Design by Holly Grundon
"All About Earth" written by Elizabeth Krych

Copyright © 2010 by Lefty's Editorial Services
All rights reserved. Published by Scholastic Inc.

SCHOLASTIC, SCIENCE SIGHT WORD READERS, and associated logos are trademarks and/or registered trademarks of Scholastic Inc.

12 11 10 9 8 7 6 5 4 3 2   10 11 12 13 14 15/0

Printed in the U.S.A.   40   Firstprinting, February 2010

SCHOLASTIC INC.

NEW YORK • TORONTO • LONDON • AUCKLAND
SYDNEY • MEXICO CITY • NEW DELHI • HONG KONG

Fast Fact

This is North America.

Our home in space is **Earth**.

It is round.

Planets

Jupiter · Mars · Earth · Mercury · Venus · Saturn · Uranus · Neptune

It is a planet.

Fast Fact

Earth

Sun

It takes one year for **Earth** to go around the Sun.

Our home in space is **Earth**.
It circles the Sun.

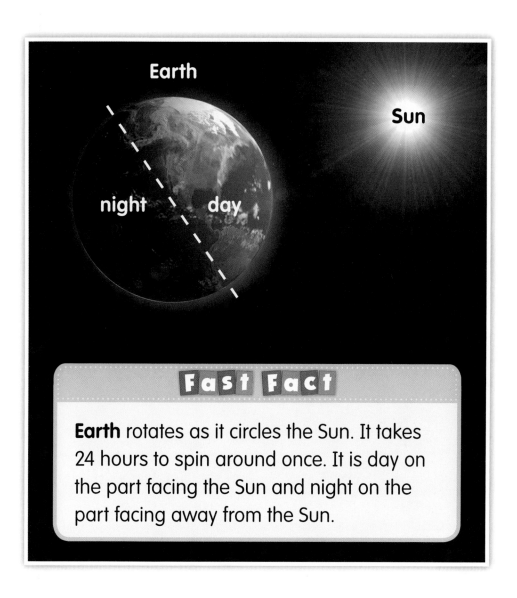

Earth

Sun

night day

Fast Fact

Earth rotates as it circles the Sun. It takes 24 hours to spin around once. It is day on the part facing the Sun and night on the part facing away from the Sun.

It **has** day and night.

Moon

Earth

Our home in space is **Earth**.

It **has** a moon.

It **has** air, too.

Our **home** in space is **Earth**.

It **has** water.

It **has** land, too.

trees

Fast Fact

There are more than 400,000 different kinds of plants on **Earth**.

flowers

Our home in space is **Earth**.
It **has** plants.

horses

Fast Fact

Some animals live on land.
Some animals live in water.

fish

It **has** animals, too.

Fast Fact

There are about seven billion people on **Earth**.

Our home in space is **Earth**.

It **has** people.

Fast Fact

Planting trees and recycling help protect the **Earth**.

Let's take good care of **our home** in space!

Sight Word Review

Point to each sight word. Then read it aloud.

Sight Word Fill-ins

Use sight words from the box
to finish each sentence.

Earth   has

home   our

1 We live on planet _____.

2 Earth is _____ home.

3 Earth _____ air, water, and land.

4 We need to take good care of our _____ in space.

All About Earth

Ask a grown-up to read this with you.

Which planet looks like a blue and green marble and is third in line from the Sun? It's Earth!

The inside of Earth is melted metal and rock. It is very, very hot. But the outside of Earth is just the right temperature for many plants and animals. Earth is surrounded by a layer of air. This is Earth's *atmosphere*. Most living things need this air to survive.

Earth spins around as if it has an invisible pole going through its center. It takes one day for it to spin completely around. But you won't fall off because a force called *gravity* holds you on Earth. And that force keeps Earth on the same path each time it circles the Sun.

Earth's path, or *orbit*, around the Sun makes our seasons. When the northern part of our planet is tilted toward the warm Sun, it's summer there! At the same time, the southern part has winter. As Earth keeps moving, the seasons keep changing. When it has made one complete trip around the Sun, the year starts over!